STRATFORD BOY

A Play in One Act for
Five Women

by T. B. Morris

Copyright © 1964 By T.B Morris
All Rights Reserved

STRATFORD BOY is fully protected under the copyright laws of the British Commonwealth, including Canada, the United States of America, and all other countries of the Copyright Union. All rights, including professional and amateur stage productions, recitation, lecturing, public reading, motion picture, radio broadcasting, television, online/digital production, and the rights of translation into foreign languages are strictly reserved.

ISBN 978-5730-1348-5

concordtheatricals.co.uk
concordtheatricals.com

FOR AMATEUR PRODUCTION ENQUIRIES

UNITED KINGDOM AND WORLD
EXCLUDING NORTH AMERICA
licensing@concordtheatricals.co.uk
020-7054-7298

Each title is subject to availability from Concord Theatricals, depending upon country of performance.

CAUTION: Professional and amateur producers are hereby warned that STRATFORD BOY is subject to a licensing fee. The purchase, renting, lending or use of this book does not constitute a licence to perform this title(s), which licence must be obtained from the appropriate agent prior to any performance. Performance of this title(s) without a licence is a violation of copyright law and may subject the producer and/or presenter of such performances to penalties. Both amateurs and professionals considering a production are strongly advised to apply to the appropriate agent before starting rehearsals, advertising, or booking a theatre. A licensing fee must be paid whether the title is presented for charity or gain and whether or not admission is charged.

This work is published by Samuel French, an imprint of Concord Theatricals Ltd.

The Professional Rights in this play are controlled by Concord Theatricals Ltd., Aldwych House, 71-91 Aldwych, London, WC2B 4HN.

No one shall make any changes in this title for the purpose of production. No part of this book may be reproduced, stored in a retrieval system, scanned, uploaded, or transmitted in any form, by any means, now known or yet to be invented, including mechanical, electronic, digital, photocopying, recording, videotaping, or otherwise, without the prior written permission of the publisher. No one shall share this title, or part of this title, to any social media or file hosting websites.

The moral right of T.B. Morris to be identified as author of this work has been asserted in accordance with Section 77 of the Copyright, Designs and Patents Act 1988.

USE OF COPYRIGHTED MUSIC

A licence issued by Concord Theatricals to perform this play does not include permission to use the incidental music specified in this publication. In the United Kingdom: Where the place of performance is already licensed by the PERFORMING RIGHT SOCIETY (PRS) a return of the music used must be made to them. If the place of performance is not so licensed then application should be made to PRS for Music (www.prsformusic.com). A separate and additional licence from PHONOGRAPHIC PERFORMANCE LTD (www.ppluk.com) may be needed whenever commercial recordings are used. Outside the United Kingdom: Please contact the appropriate music licensing authority in your territory for the rights to any incidental music.

USE OF COPYRIGHTED THIRD-PARTY MATERIALS

Licensees are solely responsible for obtaining formal written permission from copyright owners to use copyrighted third-party materials (e.g., artworks, logos) in the performance of this play and are strongly cautioned to do so. If no such permission is obtained by the licensee, then the licensee must use only original materials that the licensee owns and controls. Licensees are solely responsible and liable for clearances of all third-party copyrighted materials, and shall indemnify the copyright owners of the play(s) and their licensing agent, Concord Theatricals Ltd., against any costs, expenses, losses and liabilities arising from the use of such copyrighted third-party materials by licensees.

IMPORTANT BILLING AND CREDIT REQUIREMENTS

If you have obtained performance rights to this title, please refer to your licensing agreement for important billing and credit requirements.

CHARACTERS

(in the order of their appearance)

JOAN SHAKESPEARE
MARY SHAKESPEARE
MARION HACKET
LADY JOYCE LUCY
ANNE HATHAWAY

The action of the Play passes in the kitchen of John Shakespeare's house in Henley Street, Stratford-upon-Avon

Time—October 1582

FOR
JENIFER HANSCOMB

AUTHOR'S NOTE

Lady Lucy is portrayed as a kneeling child on her parents' tomb at Tenbury, and also in effigy with her more notorious husband at Charlcote. Her epitaph lacks nothing of praise: "When all is spoken that can be saide, a woman so furnished and garnished with vertu as not to be bettered and hardly to be equalled by any. As shee lived moste vertuously shee died moste godly. Set down by him who best did know what hath byn written to be true, Thomas Lucye."

Sir Thomas Lucy was a time-server and a persecutor of Catholics, responsible for a number of executions, including several members of Mary Shakespeare's (Arden) family in 1584. He was said to have been the cause of Shakespeare's leaving Stratford, and he was almost certainly the butt of Shakespeare's wit as Justice Shallow. Was he a man to rely on for the truth? Or was his praise of his wife's virtues only the fashion of the age?

I have supposed that, with such a husband, Joyce Lucy must have been a lady of strong personality to have achieved that epitaph. Such a lady, perhaps, as I have imagined here.

T. B. M.

STRATFORD BOY

SCENE—*The kitchen of John Shakespeare's house in Henley Street, Stratford-upon-Avon. A morning in October 1582. The setting may be a simple one. A door R leads to the entrance lobby and cobbled yard and a door L leads to the rest of the house. There is a window R of C in the back wall; a fireplace is imagined in the "fourth wall". A dresser stands L of the window, on which are a few pieces of pottery and pewter, wooden spoons, a pastry-board and a rolling-pin. (The window is optional so if it is omitted the dresser should stand back C) A kitchen table is C with stools R, L and below it; on the table is a basket or bowl of cooking apples, a dish and a knife. A small table stands below the door R on which is a bowl of old-fashioned autumn flowers and foliage. A wooden armchair is set down R facing the imaginary fireplace. A string of onions may hang on the wall together with a bunch or two of herbs and possibly an old sword and Will's home-made bow and arrows.*

If desired the setting may be elaborated with a low, leaded casement window, doors with wooden latches and bobbins, an open fireplace with irons in one of the side walls, the armchair or settle would stand above this fireplace; such items as a leather black-jack and iron candlesticks may be added. There may also be a chest which could take the place of the small table down R. Furniture at that time was scarce and crudely made.

When the CURTAIN *rises a door is heard to slam loudly off* R. JOAN SHAKESPEARE, *a girl of about 20, is sitting* R *of the table with her head on her arms, sobbing.* MARY SHAKESPEARE, *a refined and spirited woman of about 40, enters* L. *She has a bowl of dough for pastry-making.*

MARY (*placing her bowl on the table*) Now what's to do, Joan?

JOAN (*tearfully*) Father! He boxed my ears—for no cause,

Mother. I only said—about Will ... (*She breaks off, sobbing*)

MARY (*kindly, putting an arm about Joan*) I'll warrant 'twas about Will. Your brother's all your care—but you must remember that, to your father, he's only one of many cares. (*She sighs*) Though perhaps the chief. His doings are a sore trial to us.

JOAN (*looking up*) But he's only a boy ...

MARY. Eighteen. 'Tis more than time he was settling to his work, not loitering about the meadows and wasting his time in verse-making. Or worse, in the pranks and mischief of those young bully-rooks he makes company with.

JOAN (*rising and facing Mary*) Work—at butchering calves and sheep? Is that work for him? (*She begins to peel apples*)

MARY. 'Tis part of your father's business, and Will's his eldest son. 'Twill be long before Gilbert will be grown to any use, and longer for Richard and Edmund. (*She goes to the dresser and fetches the pastry-board and rolling-pin which she places on the table, making her piecrust during the following dialogue*)

JOAN. But it's not Will's work! It's not—and you know it's not! You've seen how different he is from the rest of us, ay, and everyone else in Stratford or anywhere about. He gets it from your side, Mother—from the Ardens—his dreams and all his love of tales and travels. You know it ...

MARY (*gently, not displeased*) I know nothing of the kind, and I'll hear nothing against your father.

JOAN. Oh, Father's a man of business, counting the pence—*and* with a temper. (*She rubs her ear ruefully*) But you're the one who could inspire a poet to think of romance and high doings.

MARY. Enough, Joan! It's time you learned, poppet, that there's little romance in the world today—at least, in England, which is all of it we're like to know. High chivalry went out with the Wars of the Roses, and what a man must consider now is how to pay his debts. That's what your father must think of, and hard enough things are. Doubly hard for a man who has been the first citizen of Stratford. (*She sighs*) And there are blacker things ... (*She breaks off*)

JOAN. What blacker things?

MARY. No matter to you, child. (*Earnestly*) Only, if you have any influence with your brother, beg him to have more care not to draw notice upon himself. Or on us.

JOAN. But, Mother, that is what he means to do! He'll have all men notice him and his verse, he says. He'll be high . . .

MARY (*interrupting, caution forgotten in a rush of fear*) Too many have been high—on the gallows at Tyburn or Warwick.

JOAN (*frightened*) Gallows? But Will has done nothing to —bring him to hanging?

MARY (*regretting the words; soothingly*) No, no, child! Forget it. I spoke hastily—and, indeed, your brother's enough to shake the patience of the holy angels.

JOAN. It's Father's fault! Why wouldn't he let Will go with the players when he wanted to? He'd make plays for them—great plays! I know it! He's told me of them— often . . . He wants London, or foreign parts . . .

MARY. Your father has said that these players, however they may bear the badges of my Lords of Leicester, Worcester or Nottingham—even her Majesty's—are not fit company for Will.

JOAN. But Father had them here, those years ago when he was Bailiff, and licensed them to play at *The Swan* and *The Bear*. Ay, and was foremost in watching them himself.

MARY. That's as may be. But to trust Will with them on the roads and in London is another matter.

JOAN (*wistfully*) London must be a great and glorious place, with the Queen and the processions . . .

MARY (*interrupting*) And the plague! Can be bad enough here, as we know. But in London, with such a press of bodies, 'tis like a burning brand among ripe wheat.

JOAN (*quietly*) And must a man stay at home because he fears to venture out and catch the plague? Is that what you think, Mother? I don't believe it! You're not like that, not as I know you. I've heard you, often enough since Father's troubles began, giving him courage to go on. In your heart you'd encourage Will.

MARY. You talk too much for a child who understands too little. As for Will—I tell you: try and persuade him to mend his roistering ways. There are grave reasons for it, believe me.

JOAN (*facing Mary; deliberately*) Mother! If I talk too much, you talk either too much or too little. You hint at something of fear, but won't say what it is. We must not draw notice on ourselves—and why not? Father's ever held a good name here, even though money has been scarce of late. And you—who in Stratford is more respected? As for Will's tricks and mischiefs, they're no more than a feather stirred on the wind.

MARY (*gravely*) They've brought him already to High Cross stocks, Joan, with young Hamnet Sadler.

JOAN. Because old Keeper Burnell told lies about them poaching on Charlcote ground. But they weren't there—Will said they weren't! I'd believe him against a dozen Burnells and that crabbed Sir Thomas Lucy thrown into the bargain!

MARY. S'sh! You must have care, even here! Who knows, nowadays, whether a man's very house is safe? I tell you, child—and you must tell our Will and make him see the truth of it—we must go quietly and do no more than our own business, and that without offence to any. And no ill mention of Sir Thomas and his like. He's a Justice of the Peace, remember.

(*A knocking is heard off* R. MARY *starts on hearing it*)

MARION (*calling; off* R) Mistress Shakespeare!
MARY (*with a gesture of warning to Joan*) Who's there?
MARION (*off*) Marion Hacket!
MARY (*relieved*) Ah, come in, Marion!

(MARION HACKET, *a kindly country-woman of middle age, enters* R)

Good day to you, Gossip! You find us busy.

MARION. Give ye good day—and you, too, my pretty. What? The two o' ye to one poor pie, and that but of apples? Marry! you're enough to overlay it, like two nurses to one brat. (*She laughs boisterously*)

(*The others make a pretence of joining her, but they are still uneasy*)

MARY. Sit you down. Joan shall fetch you a cup of our ale, and you shall see how it matches with yours.

(MARION *sits in the chair.*
JOAN *takes a mug from the dresser and goes off* L. MARION *gives a significant glance at her back*)

(*She goes on, not quite concealing nervousness*) What news from Wilmcote, Marion?

MARION (*garrulous, but herself showing uneasiness now*) Why, what should there be but what there always is? More bad than good, as ever, though the Lord sends it. Young Beth Ruddle—you mind her, the one with the squint?

MARY. Yes. What of her?

MARION (*a flood of speech covering her true purpose*) Oh, what you might expect. Got put in the family way by a young spark who's run off to Milford Haven and took ship. Harry Whatcott's wife ha' been blessed with twins and a quinsy all, as you may say, together. Farmer Morgan's great sow has farrowed no more than three little runts when from her size he expected near a score. And he accuses old Gossip Melworthy of overlooking the beast.

MARY. That poor soul! Ursula Melworthy never did aught but good to her neighbours, with those simples of hers. Morgan must be made to leave such nonsense. These tales, once started . . . (*She breaks off with a shiver*) God knows where they lead!

MARION (*shrewdly*) You are—troubled?

MARY (*with a quick gesture of repudiation*) But for her—and for all who suffer from evil and careless tongues. (*Angrily*) Tell Morgan his sow is too gross and should be killed and eaten—if, indeed, teeth can now be got into her. He should buy another for his breeding, not pester old Ursula to her death—and *that* death! (*She shivers again*) But, as my man could tell you, Morgan was never a good farmer. Perhaps my cousin, Edward Arden, might talk to him.

MARION (*strangely*) Edward Arden? (*She pauses thoughtfully, then goes on in a hurry*) Never fear, I'll talk to Morgan when I next get nigh him. I'll show him who'll be first in the ducking-stool if he dares raise a finger, or flap tongue, against Ursula. Ay, the women around our way are strong enough, together, to duck a few men and show 'em who's mistress of common sense.

MARY (*suddenly bleak*) And afterwards—he'll go to the Commissioners and they'll believe him. And you know how much chance Ursula will have then. From malice, simple mischief, superstition, or but to curry favour with Sir Thomas Lucy, the women may change their tale. And Ursula will drown—or worse.

(*They look at each other, both serious now.*

JOAN *enters* L *with a mug of ale and a plate of cakes which she takes to Marion*)

MARION (*pulling herself together*) Thanks, my dear. (*She takes the mug*) Well, here's health to the Queen's majesty and all with truth in 'em! (*Chuckling*) And that's safe enough for any toast in any company—ha? (*She drinks and smacks her lips*) None so bad, Gossip, none so bad!

MARY. I learned to brew at Wilmcote.

JOAN (*returning to peeling the apples*) What's this about Mistress Melworthy?

MARY. Nothing for your ears, child. A silly rumour must be scotched—as I would all rumour could be.

MARION (*dryly*) Ay. I doubt not you'd sleep sounder if there were no tongues to babble. How's the Bailiff?

MARY. No longer Bailiff, as you know well enough.

MARION. And a great shame, to be sure! There's no man better filled the office, and a-many of us look to the day when he'll be back in's seat at the Guildhall. (*She gives Mary a significant glance, with a covert gesture towards Joan when the girl is not looking*)

(MARY *understands that Marion has something to say*)

MARY (*pretending suddenly to remember*) Joan—there was that basket of quinces I promised Mistress Archer. She'll be ready for them. Find a dozen or so from the shed and take them to her, child. From among the best—not the windfalls.

JOAN. Yes, Mother. I'll just finish these apples.

MARY. Go now. I'll see to the apples. I mind she wanted to make her jelly today.

JOAN. Tomorrow, 'twas, but no matter—(*dryly*) if you want to talk what I am not to hear.

(JOAN *gives Mary an understanding glance and goes off* L, *saying as she goes*)

I'll not hurry back.

MARION (*chuckling*) Why, there's a young cockatrice!

MARY. She's sharp enough. Would her brother had as much sense. (*She rises, goes to the door* L, *looks off, then returns to face Marion*) Now, Marion, out with it. What have you been hinting that you fear to say?

MARION. I'm y'r friend, Mary Shakespeare, as you know well enough. And friend to your good man . . .

MARY. Who questions it? But you've news . . .

MARION. No. Nothing certain. Nothing but a discomfortable tangle of tales and twaddles—yet I thought a word might not come amiss.

MARY. To do with the Ardens of Parkhall? You spoke Cousin Edward's name strangely.

MARION. Ay. About them. But nothing direct, as you may say. (*She rises and moves close to Mary, speaking in a lower voice*) Except from my young Simon. You mind he's a groom at Charlcote?

MARY. Well?

MARION. He's heard talk of Sir Thomas Lucy with Parson Griffin. Just scraps of talk—but Simon's a good boy with his ears and noddle. It seems they're waiting the first excuse to search Parkhall—as well as other places—for books of the forbidden religion.

MARY (*softly; crossing herself*) Mother of God, help us!

MARION. Naught definite, but they wait occasion. And I fear they'll not have to wait long, mad as your Cousin Somerville is. Mad as his mother, the poor man, and like to run wild at any minute with a dagger for the Queen.

MARY. I would he could be restrained as his mother is.

MARION. There's this bee in his bonnet that he must kill the Queen to revive the old religion. Well, they've taken the powder and ball from his pistols, and his wife holds the purse.

MARY. Poor Cousin Margaret! I pray for her—and for

all of us. We take all care, Edward Arden and I, and pay our fines regularly for not going to church. As to the rest, we are as discreet as may be. No-one has questioned us till now. Ay, 'tis John Somerville who'll make the danger—and for us, too. He—and our Will.

MARION. Will? But your boy makes no threats against the Queen.

MARY. No. But he and his feather-headed fellows make jest at Sir Thomas and steal his birds and hares—even deer.

MARION. They're no deer of Lucy's, not at Fulbrook where those young men go. You know the place belonged to Sir Francis Englefield before he was forced to fly overseas, and Lucy stole it. Lucy's the thief.

MARY (*with a quick glance about her*) Speak not so loud, Marion. We all know that, but who's to say it here? (*Impatiently*) Ah, I rage at the thought that we, too, must toady to this Lucy! The whole county's in his greedy hand—his and Leicester's! (*She moves about restlessly*) I tell the others—and you—to keep their thoughts to themselves, yet 'tis sometimes more than I myself can do. I wasn't bred for toadying. 'Fore God, there are times when I could go out to the Cross and raise my voice with any. Lucy's a thief and a time-server. My Lord of Leicester is a murderer and adulterer, battening alike on the poor and on the Queen. And she... (*She breaks off with a gesture of frustration, struggling with herself, then goes on*) No—no! My grandsire was groom of the chambers to hers, and who can tell what a queen must do to keep her crown and the country's freedom? She must have our loyalty.

MARION. Ay! Her grandsire married the Yorkist girl and stopped the squabbles of the great. But 'tis a poor land where some can pray only in secret and the shadow of the gallows. I was never much of a one for prayers, and willing enough to repeat what parson told me to. As for books, forbidden or otherwise, I was never scholar enough to read 'em. But my gorge rises when such as Lucy shall order us...

(*She is interrupted by a clatter of two horses' hooves on the cobbles outside, to* R. *The horses stop, then trample on the cobbles, one specially restless.* MARY *is tense.* MARION *goes to the window and looks cautiously off, or to the entrance* R *if there is no window*)

(*She starts and darts back to Mary, whispering*) Mercy o' God! We've talked o' the Devil and here's his wife! 'Tis Lady Lucy!
MARY (*pulling herself together*) Easy! It may be nothing but a need for gloves from my husband's shop.

(*They stand together, tense, listening*)

JOYCE LUCY (*off* R; *an authoritative voice against the noise of the horses' hooves*) His head, boy—get his head! Think you I want to alight sprawling? Satan's got the beast this morning! Now tie the reins to the ring and help me down! Whoa, you spawn of Beelzebub! Steady here! No, mooncalf—your hand under my foot! God ha' mercy! That I should be doubly plagued—with a curst mount and a mammering page! (*A great sigh as she alights*) Haah! Now knock on the door.

(*Knocking is heard off* R)

Enough, enough! No need to beat it down!
MARION. I'd best be off.
MARY (*quickly, quietly*) No. Stay out there in the washhouse. (*She gestures* L) Hear what she has to say. It may be something they could know at Parkhall.

(MARION *moves* L, *then remembers, hastily returns, grabs up the tankard and cakes and goes off* L.
MARY *goes off* R. *There follows the sound of a door opening, off* R)

JOYCE (*off*) Give ye good day, Mistress Shakespeare.
MARY (*off*) Good morrow, my Lady. Is it gloves you need? My husband is . . .
JOYCE (*off; interrupting*) No. Not today. (*Chuckling*) Master Shakespeare makes them so well they wear not out. (*More seriously but pleasantly enough*) No—it is with you I'd speak.
MARY (*off*) Pray you come in.

JOYCE (*off*) Gramercy!
MARY (*off*) If your Ladyship would come to the kitchen ... The maid is raising dust, yet, in the parlour. This way.

(LADY JOYCE LUCY, *a lady of 50, kindly, not without humour, but direct in speech and obviously a personality to be reckoned with, enters* R. *She wears a riding-habit and hat, and carries a crop and gloves.*
MARY *follows her on*)

JOYCE. I ask your pardon for so early a call. But—it seemed—h'm!—as well. And I am one who makes up her mind and acts at once—(*with a faint chuckle*) as Sir Thomas knows.

MARY. You are welcome at any hour. Had I expected you, I'd have put Tib to work earlier. She's slow, but maids aren't what they were. Be seated, my Lady.

(JOYCE *sits in the armchair.* MARY *stands behind her for a moment, showing some uneasiness*)

JOYCE. I thank you. Make no apology. I like kitchens. Indeed, I spend much of my time in my own at Charlcote—where I'll vow I make a better showing than my cook. 'Tis as you say, they are not what they were. All gadding and no elbow-grease—a touch too light for the beeswax and too heavy for the pastry, ha? And, speaking of that, d'you know any good young maids of twelve or up, who might benefit from sound training in kitchen, stillroom or chambers?

MARY (*somewhat relieved*) Ah! ... There's young Kate Clinton and Nan Shaw, both of good, clean homes. I've heard their mothers will put them out to service. If your Ladyship could wait a moment or two, I could send Tib with a message ...

JOYCE. No matter. I know their homes and can go to them afterwards. (*With some hesitation*) 'Twas not on that account I came.

MARY (*trying to hide a sudden fear*) No? But may I offer you some refreshment? A cup of ale? Some cowslip wine?

JOYCE. Neither—I thank you. Come and sit down with me. I would have a word—as a friend.

MARY. Your Ladyship is very kind. (*She moves a stool and sits facing Joyce*)

JOYCE. Kind? (*With a little laugh*) But with reason behind it. I am the one who asks a favour of you.

MARY. A favour? Anything I can do, surely ...

JOYCE. H'm! (*She plays with her gloves, as if wondering how to begin*) You know, Mistress Shakespeare, these are the very gloves your good man made for me a year ago. If every man would do such work, caring so well to do it, England would be a better place.

MARY. He—takes pride in his work. (*But she is waiting for something less pleasant than compliment*)

JOYCE. I've heard that his affairs have not prospered so well of late.

MARY. Trade is bad.

JOYCE. He had to mortgage the Wilmcote estates he got from marrying you?

MARY (*with a faint edge to her voice*) That was four years ago.

JOYCE. And he has now no seat on the Council.

MARY (*starting to her feet with a show of pride*) Because he has been unable to pay his poor relief levies, he has—he has been too proud to attend their meetings. That is why he has lost his seat.

JOYCE. Sit down. Pride is a good thing until it grows to a sin, which it will not with you, I am sure. And you, an Arden, have a right to be proud. Believe me, I would give you no offence, and come now—as I said—friendly.

MARY (*sitting*) Friendly? (*She is puzzled*)

JOYCE. And will prove it. I think Master Shakespeare has another reason for absenting himself from public affairs —that he wishes, by avoiding notice, not to be compelled to take the oath of the Queen's supremacy.

MARY (*angrily*) The Queen has no more loyal subject.

JOYCE. True! (*Dryly*) Except as to spiritual matters. He would not wish to acknowledge her Majesty as absolute head of the church.

MARY. That oath is not pressed on—all citizens. There are—exceptions—so we pay our fines.

JOYCE. There have been. I hope there will be. And I

have said nothing of this to Sir Thomas or anyone else. Nor shall do. But conditions are changing, and—I've spoken of this to point what I am going to say. (*She pauses; then*) You have more than one son?

MARY. I have four. The youngest is asleep. Gilbert and Richard are at school. And Will, the eldest . . . (*She hesitates*)

JOYCE. The eldest. He will be helping his father, no doubt. He's grown beyond schooling.

MARY. I should have wished him to Oxford, but . . . (*She breaks off with a gesture*) Yes, my Lady, he's almost a grown man. Eighteen last April.

JOYCE. Master Shakespeare is glad of him?

MARY (*after hesitation*) No. He is not.

JOYCE. Ha?

MARY. Will—doesn't apply himself as he should. He's restless—a fault with young men, and—oh, I pray he'll grow to it. (*She stops again, then goes on, more directly*) Be good enough to give me your true reason for coming here.

JOYCE. It is about this eldest son of yours. It seems he is one of a band of young men; no more than high-spirited, perhaps, seeking what adventure they may find close home, but—thoughtless with it.

MARY (*tense*) Well?

JOYCE. Sir Thomas's head keeper, Burnell, has made many complaints . . .

MARY (*interrupting*) Master Burnell is ever full of complaints—ever was—and curst with it.

JOYCE (*with a dry chuckle*) So I gather. And myself, could I choose between the keeper and the lads, should choose the lads. But, like you, Mistress Shakespeare, I am a wife and —under God—subject to my husband. (*She chuckles again*) And his whims.

MARY. Forgive me if I scarcely understand you.

JOYCE. Patience! I come to it. There are these matters of the poaching of a bird here, a rabbit there—or more, mayhap, even to Sir Thomas's venison.

MARY. D'you come to accuse Will of deer-stealing?

JOYCE. No, no! I accuse no-one. These are, perhaps, no more than tales grown out of Burnell's spleen. And 'tis a matter between the boys and the keepers. If they're caught, they're for punishment and they know it. But—there's another and more serious matter which is not a tale.

MARY (*very anxious now*) Another?

JOYCE. Your son writes verses, I've heard.

MARY. Ay. Wastes his time at that, as in other dreaming follies.

JOYCE (*taking a rough-torn piece of paper from a pocket*) Would these lines be his? They are the last of many which those young rampallians have pinned to Charlcote gates. (*She hands the paper to Mary*) And it is I who, on account of them, must endure Sir Thomas's tantrums at close quarters.

MARY. This is a fair hand.

JOYCE. The hand's fair enough. 'Tis the words.

MARY (*reading aloud*)
"If Lucy is Loozy, as some folk miscall it,
Then Lucy is Lowsy whatever befall it."

JOYCE. It mocks the pikes—the luces—on my husband's coat-of-arms. And you, a lady born, know that is no good thing.

MARY. Indeed, my Lady, 'tis a very ill thing, and cullion's behaviour. But this is no writing of Will's. This may be read with ease. Will's hand is vile, crabbed and difficult. Many's the time I've been at him to amend it—but he says the matter set down is of more importance than the manner of writing it.

JOYCE. 'Tis not his hand, then. Is the verse his?

MARY. How should I know? They write, more than one of them, so much nonsense.

JOYCE. This goes deeper than nonsense.

MARY. I agree. And, if Will made the lines, I would he were not too high-grown for whipping.

JOYCE. D'you know whose is the hand?

MARY (*after a moment's hesitation*) No.

JOYCE (*with a quizzical glance*) I wonder?—but I'll not press that. I came to ask that you would use your influence with Master Will, and such of his friends as you know, to season their high spirits with a thought of discretion. More than once, of late, Sir Thomas has been near an apoplexy—and, as you may be aware, he is not a patient man. Now I

—can laugh at this. (*She takes back the paper*) Ay, even though I know it means ructions at the dinner-table. But he cannot. And he has power, Mistress Shakespeare, since he was made Commissioner last year, with warrant to investigate the lives and religious practice of the people here. (*She pauses, looking at Mary*) I would not wish that he should be goaded to—a too strict use of that power.

MARY (*pretending not to understand*) What? Against boys for skylarking?

JOYCE. No. Against their elders for—papistry.

MARY (*softly*) Ah!

(JOAN *enters* L. *She is angry*)

(*She gestures her off*) Presently, Joan! I've business with her Ladyship.

JOAN (*curtly*) I heard the business! (*To Joyce*) So Sir Thomas sends you to threaten us?

JOYCE. No-one sends me.

MARY (*to Joan*) 'Tis no such thing. You misheard . . .

JOAN (*interrupting*) I heard one word that was enough. Papistry—a hanging word, it seems, now.

MARY (*urgently*) Joan! You must not . . .

JOAN (*stopping her with a gesture*) But why should it be? Those who like not to follow the new religion may stay away from church, if they pay their fines. Our fines are paid, however hard the task of getting the money. So what of that?

JOYCE. Peace, child! I like your spirit—ay, and your brother's, though his needs something of taming. A falcon is of little use without jesses. Take that t'your heart and remember it. I come to beg your mother to use her influence with your brother, so that he gives up these follies—before it is too late.

JOAN. Too late?

JOYCE (*rising*) It would not be unnatural for Sir Thomas to be—ah!—forced to consider a more careful execution of his duties. And an enquiry might bring questions difficult to answer.

JOAN. You mean—because a few teasing boys make him angry, Sir Thomas would proceed against their families?

JOYCE. Against your family. If a few must be made an example, who better than Shakespeares and Ardens?

JOAN (*hotly*) Then God preserve you, madam, with such a husband!

MARY. Hold your tongue, Joan! Are you determined to ruin us all? (*To Joyce*) I ask your Ladyship to pay no heed to her. Children speak out now against their elders in a way they'd never have dared when I was a child. And she has not rightly understood you.

JOYCE (*smiling*) You need not fear that what she has said to me will go any further—except, I hope, her prayer to God for my preservation. That, I doubt not, I need. (*Moving to Joan and patting her arm; chuckling*) Though for my sins more than Sir Thomas, who is well enough as concerns myself. But I don't write ribald verses on him, nor take his game. (*Moving to Mary; taking her hands*) And believe that I come in kindness—to warn you. We want no mischief that may be avoided.

MARY. I understand—and thank you.

JOYCE. With your permission, I'll leave the horses outside your house awhile. 'Tis but a few steps to see these maids. Clinton and Shaw, you said?

MARY. Yes.

JOYCE. Good day to you.

(MARY *hurries to open the door* R *for* JOYCE, *then follows her off.* JOAN *goes to the window or the door* R *and glances off. One of the horses stamps restlessly.*

MARION *enters stealthily* L, *looking scared*)

JOAN (*angrily*) The old harridan! To dare to come here and threaten, because old lousy Thomas is angered . . .

(MARY *enters* R, *hearing the above*)

MARY (*curtly*) Will you have done, you little fool? Mischief, she said, and that's the word for it. I'd ha' given you credit for more sense! After my warning, too.

JOAN. She drove me to it, with her arrogance! Because she's married to a knight and justice, and he owns Charlcote and what more he may get his hooks on, we must make reverences and go humbly? No! The Arden blood is as good as Lucy's—better! Ay, and the Shakespeares', too!

MARY. Joan, Joan! You're too like your brother—too fiery-spirited. Jumping before you think, far less look. Lady Lucy came here in kindness. She put herself to some trouble—risk, belike—trying to save us from worse trouble.

JOAN. What worse? They'd never dare do anything against our family. As for the Ardens of Parkhall—they've been rooted there too long to be shaken out by an upstart ...

MARY (*gripping Joan's arm, shaking her*) Shut your mouth, girl! Now use your head. This is the day of the upstart. And this is what I tried to warn you of. (*To Marion*) You heard what passed?

MARION. Ay. And it goes too well with what I told you.

MARY. Get to Parkhall, Marion, and warn my cousins. Tell them to burn what dangerous books they may have, and hide the ashes—and for the love of Heaven to keep cousin Somerville's mouth shut. There must be no more of his wild threatenings, nor anything that may be construed as such. And I must get hold of Will and his father. An' he'll not listen to sense, there's but one thing for Will: we must pack him off to London, where he'll not be so easily noticed.

JOAN. He'll go to Town fast enough, and to the playhouse. You may be sure o' that. (*Enviously*) Lucky to be a boy and able to go! A plague on petticoats!

MARY. Go and find Will and bid him come here at once. Then I must take him to his father. Say nothing of what has passed. Nor of London.

(JOAN *turns to go off* R)

(*She turns to Marion*) Thanks, Marion, for your care. And now ...

(MARY *is interrupted by knocking, off* R. *All are tense.* JOAN *goes to the window, or the door* R, *and peeps off*)

JOAN (*returning; relieved*) Oh, no fears this time. 'Tis only Anne Hathaway. (*Calling*) Come in, Anne!

(*A door is heard opening, off* R.

ANNE HATHAWAY, *a girl of 26, enters* R. *She is under*

great strain and controlling herself with difficulty. The others, occupied with their own troubles, do not notice this. She is well known to them all)

MARY. Good morrow, Anne! A fine morning.
ANNE (*stiffly*) Yes. Very fine.
MARY. The leaves are at their bravery now, but they'll soon be off. How d'you like it, my dear, living at Temple Grafton?
ANNE. I'd rather be back at Shottery, if Father and Mother were still alive. But I couldn't endure my stepmother.
MARY. Poor child! Well, you must be finding a good husband now, and start a real home for yourself.
ANNE. Mistress Shakespeare, I—I've something to say...
MARY. Yes?
ANNE. If I might speak with you—alone.
MARY (*with an uneasy glance, there has been too much bad news this morning*) Why, to be sure!
MARION. Then I'll be off. Remember me to Master Sandells when you see him, Anne. (*Quietly, to Mary*) I'll not forget the message.
MARY. Thanks. Make them see things as they are. Good day to you, Marion.
MARION. Give ye good day. All will be well, we hope.

(MARION *goes off* R)

JOAN (*following Marion*) I'll go and bring Will.
ANNE (*sharply*) Not yet!
MARY (*surprised*) Why—what's this?

(*There is a pause.* MARY *and* JOAN *stand staring at Anne* ANNE *stands stiffly. Then* MARY *gestures to Joan.*
JOAN *goes off* R. *A door is heard opening, off* R)

Sit down, Anne. What ails you?
ANNE (*bleakly; staring at Mary*) What ails me? A child I do not want.
MARY. What? (*She pauses; then*) You mean you are going to have a child?
ANNE. Yes.

MARY (*after another pause; knowing the answer*) Whose?

ANNE. Your son's. (*She moves quickly to the armchair and sits, gripping the arms, staring straight before her*)

MARY. Does Will know this?

ANNE. Yes. But he doesn't know I've come to you.

MARY. So this is what has troubled him of late? (*Half to herself*) Mercy o' God, is there no end to it? When was this mischief done?

ANNE (*dully*) A night in August—a hot night. There was a moon, and he—who better to talk of love? And I—loved him.

MARY. August—and this is but October. You can't be certain.

ANNE. I am certain.

MARY. Whose was the fault? The truth, Anne! You're older than he . . .

ANNE (*still dully*) Older in years—yes. But only in years. Eight years older, and he'll come to reproach me with it. Yes, I know. But the fault—the fault? Mine as well as his, I suppose.

MARY. And what's to be done?

ANNE. He'll marry me. He's going, now, to find a priest who'll do it quietly. And a licence. Then he'd have told you—when 'twas done. (*She pauses, twisting her hands, then adds indifferently*) I've a small dowry from my father. (*Then, in deepening distress and fear*) But this will trap him here in Stratford.

MARY (*quietly*) Trapped, indeed! But not in Stratford. He must be away to London. If you must marry, you must go there with him.

ANNE. No! What should I do there, a country girl?

MARY (*bitterly*) And what will he do there, save that he has such great ideas? (*Desperately*) But he must go! He must not stay here in Stratford!

ANNE. Why must he go? Why—now?

MARY (*ignoring the question; in a sudden cruelty of despair*) An' you'll not go with him—*aah-h-h!* You'd best make shift for yourself—unmarried!

(ANNE *is tense and silent for a moment, in a clash of rivalry with Mary*)

ANNE (*quietly*) As Kate Hamnett did?
MARY (*starting*) Kate Hamnett? The maid who went into the river at Tiddington—by accident?
ANNE. No accident, according to the crowner.
MARY (*urgently*) Tell me this, Anne: have you said such a thing to Will—about going to the river? That poor girl's death has ever been much on his mind. He's dreamed of her with her clothes floating her . . . (*She pauses*) Have you threatened him with that?
ANNE (*in stony defiance*) And if I have? A girl in fear might be justified of that. As things are . . .
MARY (*interrupting; angrily*) As things are? With you, yes, and more things than you know. Oh, God help us all! Here's a coil, now, atop of everything else!
ANNE. What else?
MARY (*brutally; again ignoring the question*) It takes two to make a child. And it is for the woman to keep herself from the man—men being, as we know, the weaker creatures. And you, so much older . . .
ANNE (*bleakly*) That's the second time you've told me that I am the elder. Have I shirked my share of the blame? Oh, I could tell you how he pressed his love on me. I could make much of his temptation . . .
MARY (*interrupting; curtly*) You could make much of this: you're nearing thirty years, unmarried, eager for a husband —for any husband . . .
ANNE (*hurt*) No, no! That's unkind! Others have asked me, but I've never loved any except your Will. And he—I thought he loved me. But now I think he was only in love with love and the moon and the fancies in his head. It was his quick mind, in love with everything of life—just swept me along with the rest.
MARY (*repenting*) I'm sorry, child! I shouldn't have spoken so harshly, but—this shock—and I'm afraid . . .
ANNE. For Will?
MARY. Yes.
ANNE. I've asked you—why?

(*Two horses' hooves clattering on the cobbles can be heard. They listen*)

JOYCE (*off* R) Now take my foot, boy! Heave! Ah—you knotty-pated nayword!

(*The horses stamp violently*)

Steady now! Whoa—whoa! Hold the . . .

(*Her voice is lost in the sound of galloping hooves which quickly fade out*)

MARY. Her Ladyship's in a hurry. (*Then, to Anne*) I fear Will's pranks may bring more trouble on him—and on us.

ANNE. As a married man, he'll forget all his boy's behaviour.

MARY. Boy's behaviour—yes, boy's! And he's to be a married man—not yet nineteen and never more than scapegrace! Can't keep himself, far less you and a child. And you said—you fear he thinks you've trapped him into marriage.

ANNE. That was not what I said! He said he'd trapped himself.

MARY. If he thinks of a trap at all, 'tis clear he'll be no willing husband. Would you have him marry you for no more than duty?

ANNE (*rising; angrily*) He's promised it. I'll hold him to his promise. Or I'll not live to be shamed. Oh, I'd hoped that you would hear me in kindness . . .

MARY. In kindness—with such news?

ANNE. Is it so bad? I'm strong and can work for him. And marriage will put a stop to idle frolics, that I'll promise you.

MARY. You think, girl, that you can do what his father and I have not? You'll put a different face on this after a month of living with him. Will's an untamed hawk . . . (*Troubled*) What did she say, that woman? A falcon is no use without the jesses—the binding straps . . . So you think you'll tame him? And then—clip his wings?

ANNE. Why should I clip his wings? Is that what you'd do?

MARY. No. I know something of what he struggles against, though I've had to stifle it in myself. I'd have him fly, if such a flight were possible. More—I'd have him in London, now, facing his fortune. (*She shakes her head*)

But you, Anne—he should have seen he'll get no inspiration of you.
ANNE (*bitterly*) Only the inspiration to father a child.
MARY. That? Any tinker's doxy can give that.
ANNE (*more deeply hurt*) Tinker's doxy!
MARY (*curtly*) Ay. Giving her body. But *she'd* give more. She'd go with her man, whatever was the road. And you— you'll not go to London with Will.
ANNE. I've said I'll not! He took me here, and he shall keep me here. I couldn't abide London. I'd be no use to him there, or to myself or our child. (*Losing her anger; appealing*) Oh, he'll forget these fancies and settle to work. He loves the country, you know he does. You've heard him talk of the country things, the weeds, the flowers. Why, he'll make a very marvel o' the red spots of a cowslip flower ... He'll stay! He'll ... (*She breaks off, fighting for control, then suddenly drops on to a stool by the table, hiding her face on her arms, weeping*) By Christ's compassion, give me pity, Mother! ...

(MARY *softens and goes to Anne, putting her arms about her*)

MARY. Ay—pity! We'll all need that—but Will more than most. This is no good foundation for a marriage, girl —a bond enforced, and straps to trammel a hawk. We must pray for help ...

(*Hooves of two horses are again heard off, approaching and drawing up*)

(*Still holding Anne, she is tense, listening*) What now?

(JOAN *runs on* R, *leaving the door, if any, open*)

JOAN. 'Tis the Charlcote woman back again.

JOYCE (*off; abruptly*) Take the reins, boy! Nay, I'll not be a moment. I'll shift for myself, better than your fumbling. And then I'll give this God-forsaken beast a lesson— (*grunting as she slips from the horse*) haah!

(JOYCE *enters* R *as vigorously as a March wind; still talking*)

I'll learn him to jaunce my bones about the cobbles o' Stratford! (*To Mary*) Your pardon, Mistress. I came back with a word for you. That son o' yours ...

MARY (*bleakly*) Will—I know not what we'll do with him.

JOYCE (*briskly*) Don't fret as to that—'tis what he'll do with himself! You may be sure o' this: he'll go no man's way but his own—and God help him choose the right one. You need but look once into his eyes to see he's no ordinary man. You'll be proud o' him yet, I'll warrant. Furthermore, I'm his debtor now for saving my life. That beast o' mine has the devil in him, and, but for your Will, my neck had likely been broke by now. He perilled his own neck to stop the creature.

(ANNE, *with* MARY, *is looking at Joyce.* MARY *is still holding Anne*)

If the time comes when he should need help, bid him remember that Joyce Lucy owes him more than thanks. (*She smiles, adding dryly*) But, for now, remind him that Sir Thomas's temper is no better than that o' my horse. Give ye good day again.

JOYCE *turns abruptly and goes off* R. MARY *and* ANNE *remain still, looking after her as—*

the CURTAIN *falls*

FURNITURE AND PROPERTY PLOT

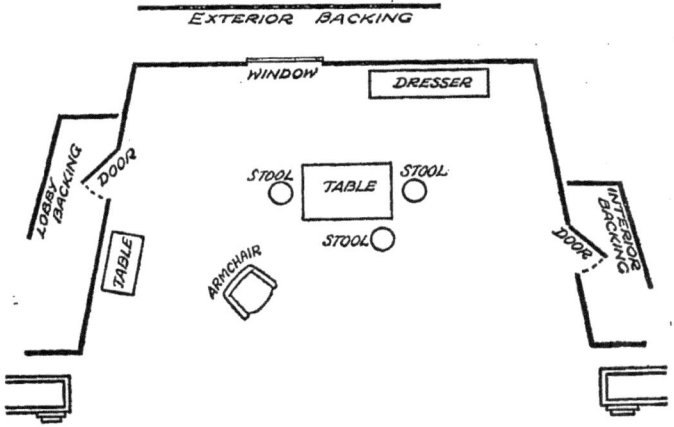

On stage: Kitchen table. *On it:* basket or bowl of apples, dish knife
Table. *On it:* bowl of autumn flowers and leaves
Wooden armchair
3 stools
Dresser. *On it:* pieces of pottery and pewter, wooden spoons, pastry-board, rolling-pin

On walls: String of onions, bunches of herbs, bow and arrows, a sword
Other dressing may be added at the discretion of the Producer

Off stage: Bowl of dough (MARY)
Plate of cakes, mug of ale (JOAN)

Personal: JOYCE LUCY: riding crop and gloves. Piece of tattered paper with verse on it (in a pocket)

LIGHTING PLOT

Property fittings required: none

Interior. The same scene throughout

THE MAIN ACTING AREAS are RC, C and LC

To open: Effect of autumn sunlight
No cues

EFFECTS PLOT

Cue 1	At the rise of the CURTAIN *Door slam off* R	(Page 1)
Cue 2	MARY: "... the peace, remember." *Knocking off* R	(Page 4)
Cue 3	MARION: "... Lucy shall order us." *Clatter of two horses' hooves off* R	(Page 8)
Cue 4	JOYCE: "... knock on the door." *Knocking off* R	(Page 9)
Cue 5	MARY goes off R *Sound of door opening off* R	(Page 9)
Cue 6	JOAN glances off R or through window *Sound of restless horse*	(Page 15)
Cue 7	MARY: "... and now ..." *Knocking off* R	(Page 16)
Cue 8	JOAN: "... Come in, Anne!" *Sound of door opening off* R	(Page 16)
Cue 9	JOAN goes off R *Sound of door opening off* R	(Page 17)
Cue 10	ANNE: "I've asked you—why?" *Sound of horses' hooves on cobbles*	(Page 19)
Cue 11	JOYCE: "... knotty-pated nayword!" *Sound of horses stamping violently*	(Page 20)
Cue 12	JOYCE: "... Whoa! Hold the ..." *Sound of galloping hooves fading away*	(Page 20)
Cue 13	MARY: "... pray for help ..." *Two horses heard approaching and drawing up*	(Page 21)

NOTE: The effect of horses' hooves can be imitated with the halves of a coconut shell or with small wooden bowls. The effect must be carefully practised, both as to the surface on which the bowls are struck and also as to timing. Lady Lucy's horse must be suggested as becoming increasingly restless and this effect may be added to by a little occasional stamping during her first period on the stage, provided this is not unduly intrusive.

www.ingramcontent.com/pod-product-compliance
Ingram Content Group UK Ltd.
Pitfield, Milton Keynes, MK11 3LW, UK
UKHW021840210426
5322IPUK00022B/397

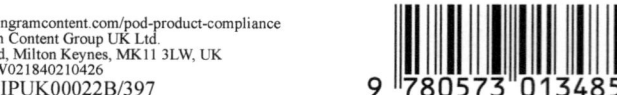